"TEACH ME YOUR WAYS, O LORD,
THAT I MAY LIVE ACCORDING
TO YOUR TRUTH!"

Psalm 86:11

- -

HOW TO USE THIS BOOK

Set aside time each day to discover...study... enjoy... learn... the Christmas story. You can study/write each verse in one day, or take a couple days to complete the "lesson."

First, look up the Scripture passage in your Bible.

 *Matthew 1:18-25*

 **QUICK TIPS** Read the entire passage listed, even though you are only copying a portion of it.

Trace the letters in the Bible verse.

 **TRACE**

=

 **WRITE**

TRACE & WRITE

"She will have son, and

"She will

you are to name him

Jesus, for he will save his

people from their sins."

Write the verse on your own.

 **QUICK TIPS** You can either trace the entire verse at once, and then write it on your own; or trace the words on one line, write it on the following line, trace the next line, write it on the following, etc.

 **QUICK TIPS** If writing the entire verse is too difficult, pick out a couple words for them to write instead.

HOW TO USE THIS BOOK

Use a dictionary, or bible concordance, to look up the definitions to the words listed.

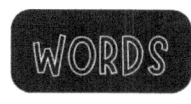 **WORDS**

"She will have a son, and you are to name him Jesus, for he will save his people from their sins." Matt. 1:21

Look up and write down the definitions to these words:

save: *to rescue from danger*

sins: *a violation of a religious or moral principle*

 **QUICK TIPS**

All the Scripture in this book is from the New Living Translation (NLT). You don't have to use that version, but it will make it easier to find and define the words in the Bible passage.

Draw a picture to illustrate the Bible verses

DRAW

His name is Jesus, & he will save us from our sin!

 **QUICK TIPS**

When you illustrate the verse, it helps you take the time to understand what the passage means.

John 3:16-17

"For this is how God

loved the world:

He gave his one and

only Son...."

WORDS

"For this is how God loved the world: He gave his one and only Son...." John 3:16

Look up and write down the definitions to these words:

love:

gave:

DRAW

Draw a picture to illustrate the Bible verses.

TRACE & WRITE

"So the Word became

human and made his

home among us."

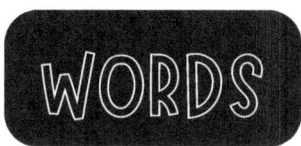

WORDS

"So the Word became human and made his home among us." John 1:14

Look up and write down the definitions to these words:

Word:

human:

DRAW

Draw a picture to illustrate the Bible verses.

TRACE & WRITE

"Because God's

children are human

beings...the Son also

became flesh and blood."

"Because God's children are human beings--made of flesh and blood--the Son also became flesh and blood." Hebrews 2:14

Look up and write down the definitions to these words:

children:

flesh and blood:

Draw a picture to illustrate the Bible verses.

Luke 1:26-33

"Don't be afraid, Mary,"

the angel told her,

"for you have found

favor with God!"

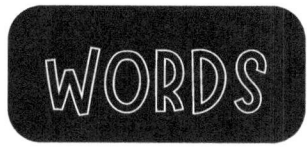

WORDS

"Don't be afraid, Mary," the angel told her, "for you have found favor with God!" Luke 1:30

Look up and write down the definitions to these words:

favor:

DRAW

Draw a picture to illustrate the Bible verses.

TRACE & WRITE

"So the baby to be

born will be holy, and

he will be called the

Son of God."

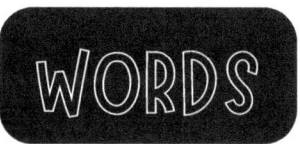

"So the baby to be born will be holy, and he will be called the Son of God." Luke 1:35

Look up and write down the definitions to these words:

holy:

Draw a picture to illustrate the Bible verses.

TRACE & WRITE

"You are blessed

because you believed

that the Lord would

do what he said."

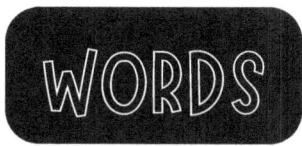 **WORDS**

"You are blessed because you believed that the Lord would do what he said." Luke 1:45

Look up and write down the definitions to these words:

blessed:

believe:

 **DRAW**

Draw a picture to illustrate the Bible verses.

TRACE & WRITE

"Oh, how my soul

praises the Lord.

How my spirit rejoices

in God my Savior!"

WORDS

"Oh, how my soul praises the Lord. How my spirit rejoices in God my Savior!" Luke 1:46

Look up and write down the definitions to these words:

soul:

spirit:

Savior:

DRAW

Draw a picture to illustrate the Bible verses.

TRACE & WRITE

"She will have a son, and

you are to name him

Jesus, for he will save his

people from their sins."

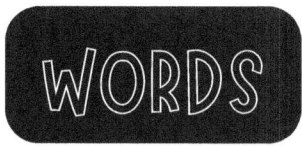**WORDS**

"She will have a son, and you are to name him Jesus, for he will save his people from their sins." Matt. 1:21

Look up and write down the definitions to these words:

save:

sins:

DRAW

Draw a picture to illustrate the Bible verses.

Luke 2:1-7

"She wrapped him

snugly in strips of

cloth and laid him in

a manger...."

"She wrapped him snugly in strips of cloth and laid him in a manger...." Luke 2:7

Look up and write down the definitions to these words:

manger:

Draw a picture to illustrate the Bible verses.

Luke 2:8-20

"Don't be afraid...! I

bring you good news

that will bring great

joy to all people."

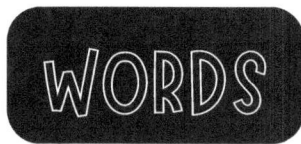

WORDS

"Don't be afraid!" he said. "I bring you good news that will bring great joy to all people." Luke 2:10

Look up and write down the definitions to these words:

good news:

joy:

DRAW

Draw a picture to illustrate the Bible verses.

TRACE & WRITE

"Where is the newborn

king of the Jews?

We saw his star as it

"rose...."

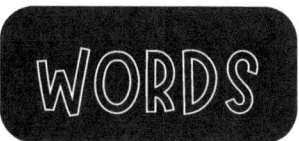
WORDS

"Where is the newborn king of the Jews? We saw his star as it rose, and we have come to worship him." Matt. 2:2

Look up and write down the definitions to these words:

king:

worship:

DRAW

Draw a picture to illustrate the Bible verses.

Isaiah 9:6–7

"Wonderful Counselor,

Mighty God,

Everlasting Father,

Prince of Peace."

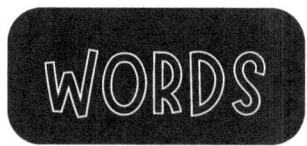

WORDS

"And he will be called: Wonderful Counselor, Mighty God, Everlasting Father, Prince of Peace." Isaiah 9:6

Look up and write down the definitions to these words:

Counselor:

Mighty:

Everlasting:

Peace:

DRAW

Draw a picture to illustrate the Bible verses.

If you need tools to help your children grow in their walk with the Lord, use this QR Code to go to

DIGGINGINTOGOD.COM